THE BIG BOOK OF TRICKS AND MAGIC

A RANDOM HOUSE BOOK

THE
BIG BOOK
OF
TRICKS
AND
MAGIC

by JAMES R. BLACKMAN

ISBN: 0-394-80632-8

CONTENTS

THE BIG BOOK OF TRICKS AND MAGIC

FOREWORD

In life there are two kinds of people: those who lead the parade and those who follow the leader. Every one of us secretly yearns to stand out from the crowd and win the admiration of our friends and family but too few of us have any idea as to how to attain this goal. Entertainment is one of the surest and most rewarding ways to popularity. The sound of laughter or the look of pleased amazement on your friends' faces at the completion of a well-executed magic trick are more than adequate compensation for the time taken to learn these simple tricks.

In addition to being a crowd pleaser, the art of magic offers other compensations. It develops quickness and a good use of your hands. It also will develop the necessary poise to address groups of people, since one of the most important things to a magician is a good line of patter to hold the audience's interest while he is completing a trick.

I am sure you will find the tricks demonstrated in this book by my son easily learned with a little practice, and magic will prove to be a very inexpensive hobby since most of the materials needed can be found in your own home.

After you have become proficient at doing the tricks you will be amazed at the amount of pleasure your friends will derive from watching you do them...but more importantly you will be astounded at the feeling of satisfaction you will have at being able to do something everyone else can't do.

JAMES R. BLACKMAN

Can you form a perfect square with these matches
by moving only one match?

THE SQUARE TRICK

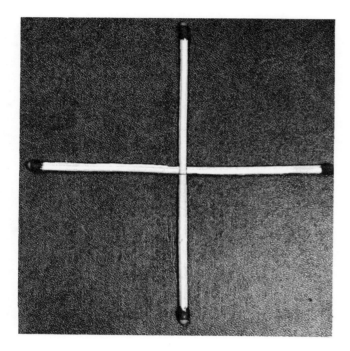

Take care to arrange
the matches exactly as
shown in the picture.

Gently move the
top match, and as you
see you will have formed
a square in the center
of the arrangement!

Materials: Four matches.

Can you make a walking
man out of the numbers
given below by making just
two straight strokes with a pencil?

The Walking Man

Write the numbers I I 0 3 0 on a piece of paper.

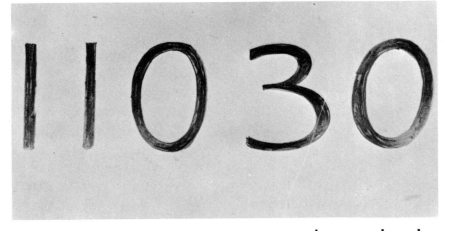

This one is easy! Using one stroke, make the
letter **H** out of the **I I**. With the second stroke,
make the letter **B** out of the **3**.

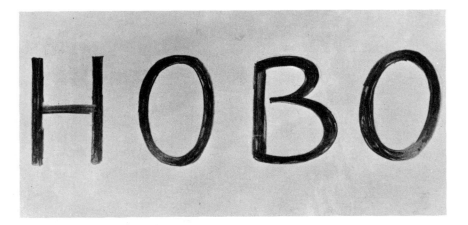

Materials: A piece of paper and a pencil.

Can you pick up an empty pop bottle with
a straw without touching the bottle?

The Straw and Bottle Trick

Materials: A dry straw and
a short stubby pop bottle.

Bend straw a little less
than one third its length,
with both ends pointing upward.

Place straw in bottle, bent
part first, holding onto the
long end. Then pull up on
straw slowly. The straw will
wedge and you can pick up the
bottle without touching it!

Can you by your magic power restore a broken
match to its original condition?

THE MIRACLE MATCH

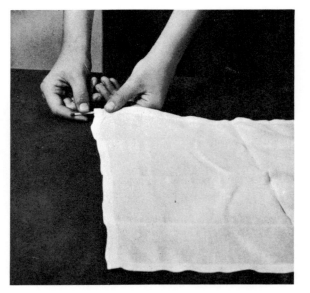

Use a large handkerchief with a wide
hem. Insert a match all the way into
the hem, so that it can't be seen.
This is done beforehand and the
handkerchief placed in your pocket.

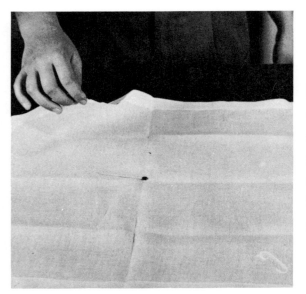

Now after announcing what you can
do, pull the handkerchief out, lay it
on a table, and place the second
match in the center. Then pick up the
corner which has the match inserted
in the hem, and start folding
all four corners.

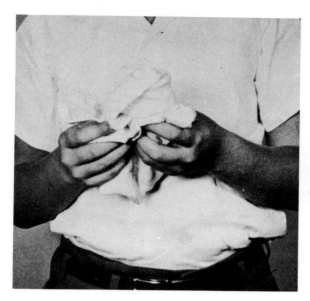

Pick up handkerchief, and when you have located the position of the match in the hem, let one of your guests feel it and break it in two.

Now shift the handkerchief in your hands a bit and utter some magic words such as "match, match, mend thyself." Then shake the handkerchief, and the whole match will fall on the table. The broken one will remain in the hem.

Materials: Handkerchief and two matches.

Can you make a silver coin weep?

THE WEEPING COIN

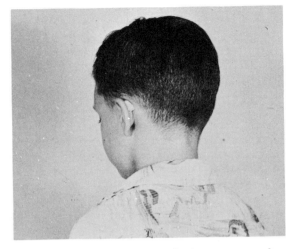

The secret of this trick is to get the piece of wet cotton behind your ear without being observed.

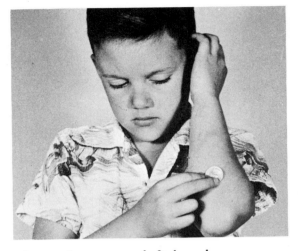

Then place your left hand over your ear and with your right hand rub the coin on your arm, making some remark about the importance of rubbing the arm.

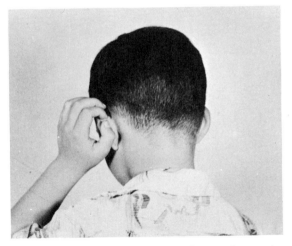

Your friends will be watching the coin and will not notice that you are picking up the wet cotton with the hand that is over your ear.

Now very quickly place the wet cotton behind the coin and squeeze it. Your friends will be amazed to see water drip from the coin. When the water stops dripping, slip the piece of cotton into your pocket or drop it out of sight. Then show your friends the coin and let *them* try to make it weep!

Materials: A silver half dollar, a small piece of wet cotton or tissue.

Can you remove the penny with your fingers without causing the match that is slanted to fall away from the upright match?

The Match and Penny Trick

Stand the cover of the match box on its side, with the scratching surface up. Sharpen the untreated end of a wooden match, and stick it in the upper side of the cover, fairly close to the end. Against the head of this match, rest the head of the second match. Hold the second one in position by placing a penny against its untreated end.

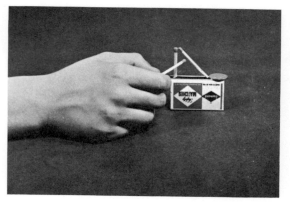

Light the third match and ignite the heads of both matches.

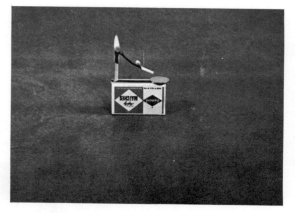

The second match will curl away from the penny, and you will be able to pick up the penny without causing the second match to fall away from the first.

Materials: Three matches, a penny, a safety-match box and a knife. For safety reasons, place match box on a fire resistant surface.

Can you balance a handkerchief on the tips of your fingers and make it rise and fall at your command?

The Balancing Handkerchief

Insert a soda straw into the hem of a handkerchief. This and the following step should be prepared ahead.

Tie a knot at the corner of the handkerchief, and push straw up to the knot. Place the handkerchief carefully in your pocket, so you don't break the straw. Now you are ready to show your friends the trick.

Materials: A handkerchief with a wide hem, and a soda straw.

Take the handkerchief from your pocket, holding the knot in one hand. With the other hand, stroke the handkerchief downward two or three times. Still holding it by the knot, bring the other hand down, grasping the lower end of the straw between the tips of the thumb and forefinger. Release your hold on the knot, and it will look as if the handkerchief is balanced upright. Make this look difficult, as if you are making a great effort at balancing the handkerchief.

By a sliding movement of the forefinger and thumb, allow the handkerchief to come down slowly, saying "Down Billy." Then say, "Up Billy." You can do this several times. At the end, throw the handkerchief into the air, catching and crumpling it up before placing it back in your pocket. If you have two handkerchiefs prepared, you can satisfy the skeptic who says, "Bet you can't do it again!"

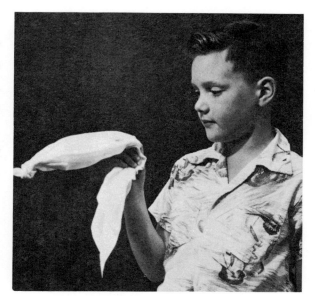

Can you make a coin appear in an empty match box?

The Matchless Matchbox

Two steps of this trick must be completed beforehand. First, open the drawer of the match box far enough so that you can wedge a coin between the cover and the end of the drawer. The second step is to slide the drawer in part way until the coin is covered.

When ready, hold up the apparently empty match box, half opened so that your friends can see inside, and say, "This box is matchless in more ways than one."

Now close the box (the coin will drop into the drawer). After a few magic words, open the box again. To your friends' surprise a coin has appeared!

Materials: A penny and a match box.

Can you snare an ice cube with a piece of string
and lift the cube from the glass?

The String and Ice-Cube Trick

Float an ice cube in a glass of water. Take a string and tie a loop in one end, then invite your friends to try their luck. They will fail, because looping the ice cube is just about impossible.

When they give up, show how it can be done. Simply let the wet loop rest on the ice cube. Sprinkle a little salt on the ice. The surface will melt and then freeze again, with the string embedded in the ice cube. (It takes a little time for the surface to freeze again, so don't be too hasty with this trick.)

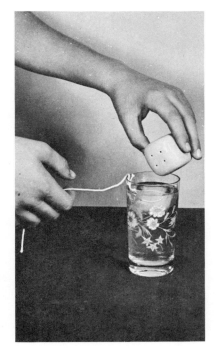

Now lift the string carefully by the free end, and you can draw the ice cube out of the glass.

Materials: Salt shaker, string with a loop, cube of ice, and a glass of water.

Can you make a pencil mark that has been placed on a cube of sugar pass mysteriously through water and onto the hand?

The Amazing Sugar Cube

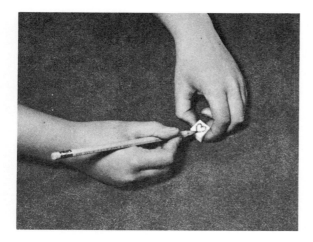

On any one side of the cube of sugar draw a heart, a number, or a cross with heavy strokes.

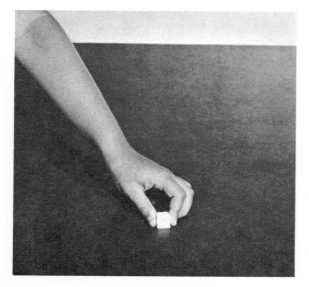

Pick up the cube and press your thumb firmly against the drawing. The mark will come off the sugar and show on your thumb. (As this is the secret of the trick, do it quickly so it will not be noticed.)

Drop cube in glass of water.

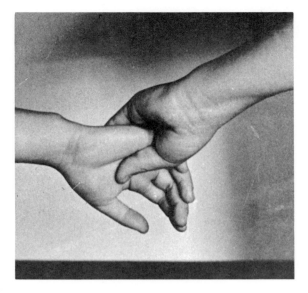

Pick up your friend's hand and quickly press your thumb firmly against the palm of his hand as you are drawing his hand toward the glass.

Place his hand over the glass of water and tell him to keep it down firmly.

Hit the glass a sharp tap with the pencil, saying, "I am now releasing the vibrations."

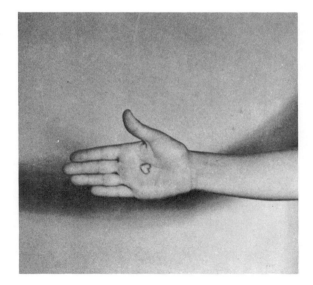

Then tell your friend to look at his hand. He will see the mark and will think it came through the water onto his hand!

Materials: Soft lead pencil, cube of sugar, three-quarters of a glass of water.

Can you remove a dollar bill from under a bottle
without touching or upsetting the bottle?

The Dollar Bill and Bottle Trick

Place the bottle upside
down on the bill, either
on a table or the
bare floor.

Roll up the bill carefully,
touching only the edges of
the bill so that your fingers
do not come in contact
with the bottle. As you roll
the bill, the bottle will be
pushed along until it is
finally off the bill.

Materials: Dollar bill and pop bottle.

Can you remove a coin from under a cup without touching the cup?

The Magician's Assistant

Place one coin on a table, put the cup over the coin, and tell your friends that you are going to remove the coin without touching the cup.

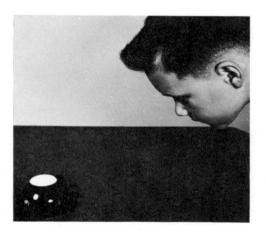

With the second coin, which you have kept concealed in your hand, tap the table from the underside just under the cup, saying, "Here is that coin."

Materials:

Two coins and a cup.

Naturally, your friend will then pick up the cup to see if the coin has disappeared. Now you quickly pick up the coin that was under the cup and say, "I told you I could pick it up without touching the cup." Your friend has unwittingly been a magician's assistant!

In this game, can you figure out how to make sure
that your opponent *always* picks the last match?

THE LAST MATCH

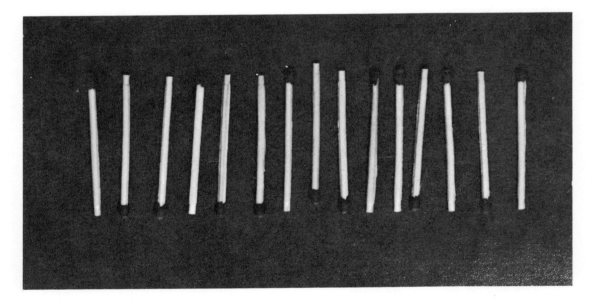

Arrange fifteen matches side by side on a table. Tell one
of your friends that you can always make him pick up
the last match, each of you alternating in picking up one,
two or three matches at a time. It doesn't matter who starts.

Materials: Fifteen matches.

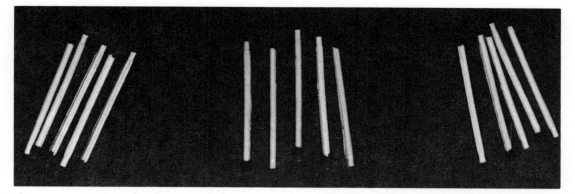

The secret of this trick is to make certain to leave five matches on the table for your opponent the third time around. Then, no matter how many matches he picks up, he will lose the game. For instance, if he picks up one, you take three, leaving the last one for him. Or if he picks up two, you take two. If he picks up three, you take one. In each case, the last match is left for him.

Following are two of the several combinations you can use to arrive at the point of leaving the five matches for your opponent.

Opponent	You	15 M
(3	1	(11
Take (2	2 Leaving	(7
(1	1	(5
	Or	
(1	2	(12
Take (2	1 Leaving	(9
(3	1	(5

Can you tell the color of a crayon without
seeing it, simply by feeling it?

THE MAGIC CRAYON

Hold your hands behind your back,
and have someone choose a
crayon of any color and place
it in your palm.

Grasp crayon in one hand and
run thumbnail of other hand over
end of crayon.

Then quickly raise your hand to
forehead and pretend to be
concentrating, at the same time
stealing a peek at the bit of crayon
on your thumbnail. After uttering
a few magic words, reveal the
color of the crayon.

Materials: Several crayons of different colors.

Can you rearrange all these glasses in alternating order—a filled one next to an empty one—by moving or touching only one glass?

The Alternating Glass Trick

The glasses must be arranged in a row in the order shown. Now pick up the fourth glass from the left and pour its contents into the first glass on the left.

Then place the emptied glass back in its original spot.

Materials: Six glasses, three of them empty and three partly filled with water. (A few drops of milk were added to the water for a clearer picture.)

Can you make a coin disappear by rubbing it into your arm?

THE MAGIC COIN

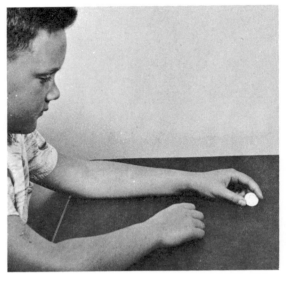

Spin a coin on the table, and announce that it is a magic coin, and that you can make it disappear by rubbing it into your arm.

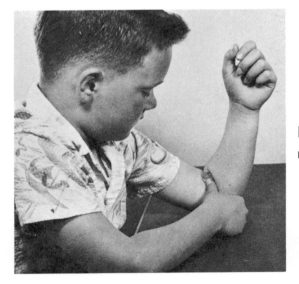

Pick up coin with your right hand and rub it against your left arm.

Take your right hand away, letting the coin fall on the table. Act surprised and say, "I guess I didn't rub hard enough." Do this again and remark, "My skin must be tough; it takes a lot of rubbing."

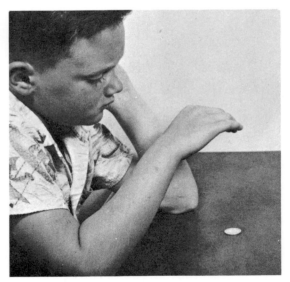

Materials: A coin.

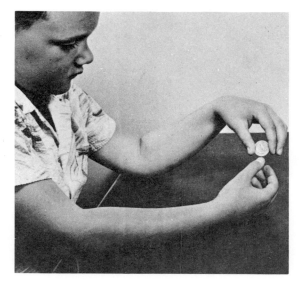

Now pick up the coin in your left hand and pretend to put it in your right, but palm it in your left hand.

Start rubbing as before, pretending you are using the coin. Meanwhile, lift your left hand and casually scratch your neck, letting the coin drop inside your shirt collar.

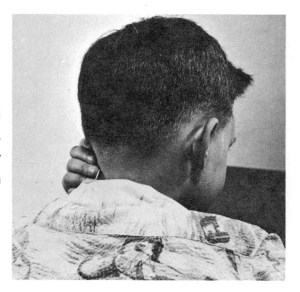

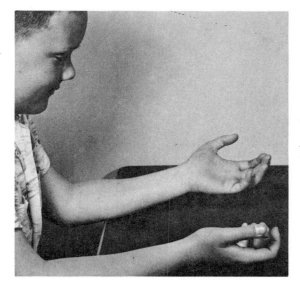

Then take your right hand away from your arm and show that the coin has vanished!

Can you remove one of the glasses
without making the match fall?

The Glass and Match Trick

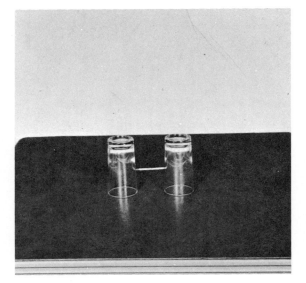

Wedge one of the matches
between the two glasses.

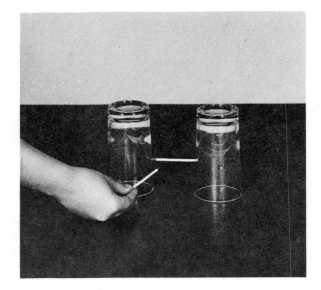

Use the second match to light
the head of the first match. As
soon as the head lights, blow
out the flame. Let cool for a
few seconds.

The match doesn't fall but
sticks to the glass, and you
can remove the other glass!

Materials: Two glasses and two kitchen matches.

Can you make four triangles, all of the
same size, with six matches?

THE TRIANGLE TRICK

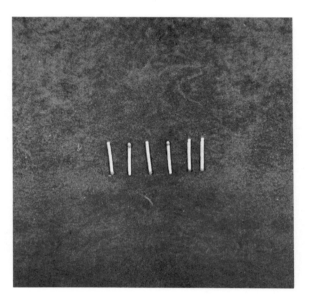

Materials: Six matches.

Lay three matches flat on the table in
the form of a triangle. Then stand
the other three on end, one in each
corner of the first triangle, and let the
other ends meet to form a tripod
or wigwam, as shown. Count them
—four triangles!

Can you make ten out of nine matches? Keep up the patter as your friends struggle to do this trick.

The Matchstick Trick

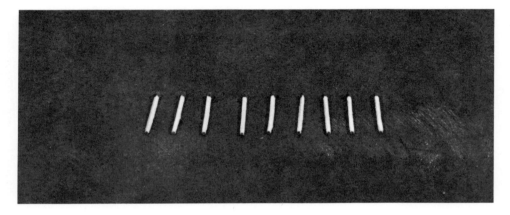

Say, "I'll make ten out of these nine matches."

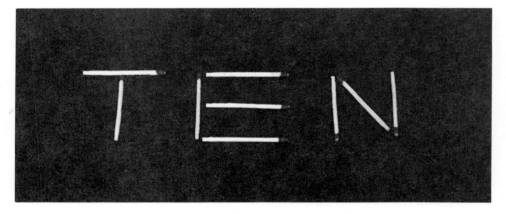

As you can see from the picture, this one is easy —once you know the trick!

Materials: Nine matchsticks (or toothpicks).

Could you tell which of these cards was touched
while you were out of the room?

THE MASTERMIND

This trick is lots of fun, and is especially good after dinner while a group is still sitting around the table. Place some cards on the table, and then ask somebody to touch one of them while you are out of the room. Tell him you will be able to pick out the one he has touched. The secret of this trick is to have a confederate (someone who knows the trick) sit next to you at the table.

When you come back, sit down, and start touching the cards one at a time. When you touch the right card, your confederate will tap you lightly on the foot. You can't go wrong! And you can do it several times before anyone catches on.

Materials: Twelve to fifteen playing cards, placed on a table as shown.

Do you want to make your friends believe you have some strange power? You will have to prepare a small box of matches beforehand, then you can do the trick on the spur of the moment.

MATCH BOX TRICK

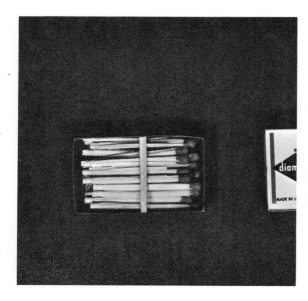

Break or cut one of the matches so that it is just long enough to wedge across the drawer of the match box (this must fit snugly as the trick depends on this wedge match.)

Insert drawer in box and put box where it will not be disturbed.

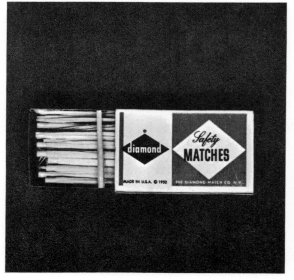

Materials: A small box of matches.

Now you are ready any time to bring out the box and tell your friends that you can make the matches stick to the inside of the box. Open the box part way (be sure the wedge match does not show) so that everybody can see there are matches in the box. Close the box.

Now turn the box upside down and pull the drawer all the way out, holding it so everyone can see you are not using your fingers to hold the matches in.

Your friends will be amazed that the matches stay in the box. To prove that the matches are still there, tap the drawer sharply against the table edge, still keeping the drawer upside down. The wedge will dislodge and the matches will fall in a heap. Pick them up (pocketing the wedge), put them in the box, and let your friends try to figure out how the trick was done!

Can you make a coin vanish into thin air?

The Vanishing Coin

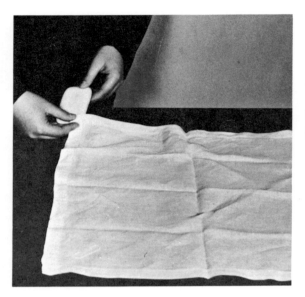

The secret of this trick is to put a small amount of soft soap on a corner of the handkerchief while no one is watching.

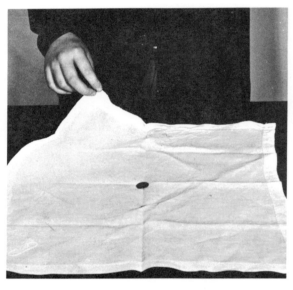

Place dime in the center of the handkerchief.

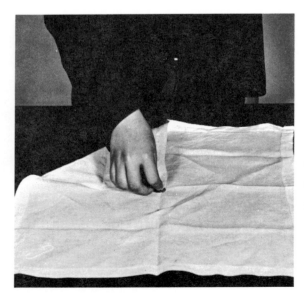

Pick up the corner nearest your right hand, which should be the corner with the soap. Then press it on the dime.

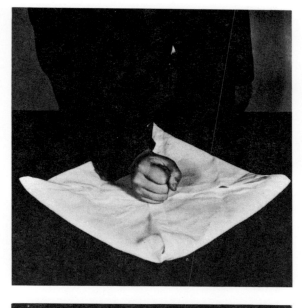

Take the other three corners of the handkerchief and fold down over the first corner. Let a person standing by feel the dime, and with that, tell him you are going to pass it right through the table. Then let your fist come down on it with a thud.

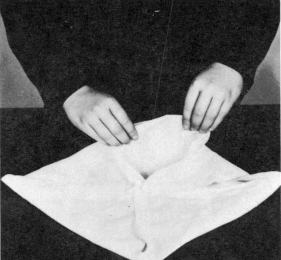

Next, place the thumbs of each hand under the folded edge, as shown.

With a quick outward movement, straighten the edge and grasp the corners. If you have done this properly the coin, which had been stuck by the soap to one of the corners, is now concealed in your right hand. Deftly pocket the coin while holding the handkerchief up for inspection. If you can keep up the patter while doing this trick, it will help.

Materials: Some soft soap, a coin and a handkerchief.

Have you ever seen a bandana that eats matches?

The Match-Eating Bandana

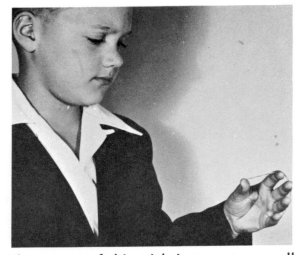

The secret of this trick is to get a small rubber band around the fingers of your left hand while no one is looking. Keep hand closed and no one will notice it.

Pick up matches with the right hand.

Bring left hand up under center of bandana. The hand is open with the rubber band around the fingers. Push matches down into palm, and pull or slide band off fingers and around matches. You will notice they are held in the bandana.

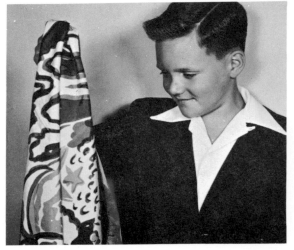

Shake bandana, and to your friends' amazement, the matches have been "eaten" by the bandana!

Materials: Small rubber band, some matches, and a brightly figured bandana.

Can you make a fork sing?

THE SINGING FORK

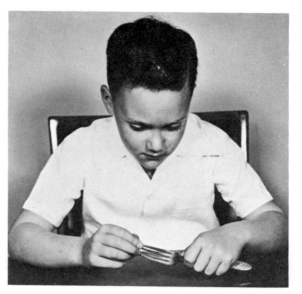

This is a perfect trick to do at the dinner table or after refreshments at a party.

As illustration shows, grasp fork in center of handle, and keep it close to but not touching the table. With the left hand, pick the prongs of the fork firmly. It will give forth a dull sound.

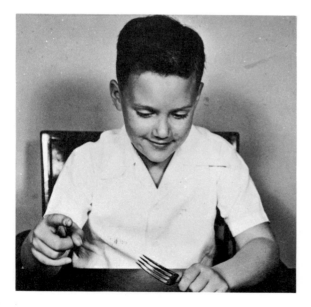

Wait a second, and then with the free hand, point to or touch any nearby object. As you do this, let the handle of the fork come to rest on the table and pick the prongs firmly once more. To your friends' amazement, the fork will sing!

Materials: Dinner fork and a table covered with a cloth.

Can you make the drawing below in one unbroken line?

THE UNBROKEN LINE

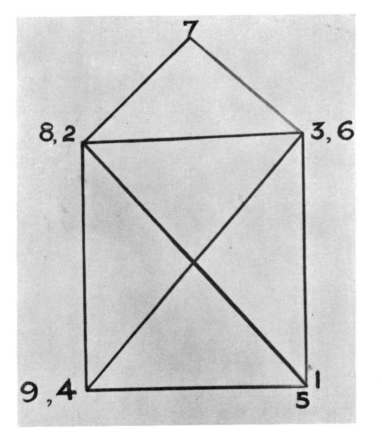

This trick is simple; there are many ways it can be done. Several persons can try it at the same time.

Do not put the numbers on the diagram. They were put in simply to show you one way the trick can be done.

Materials: A sheet of paper and pencil for each person, and the diagram shown.

Can you cut the string in two without making the cup fall?

THE HANGING CUP

Tie the string to the handle of the cup as shown and let someone hold the upper end of the string. Then state that you are going to cut the string in two and that because of your magic powers the cup will not fall.

This one is simple. Make a large loop in the string and knot it. Then snip the string in the loop, as shown, and announce, "It is cut and the cup is still hanging!"

Materials: A cup, a piece of heavy string and a pair of scissors.

Can you place all the glasses in an upright position after making three moves?

THREE GLASSES

This is an excellent but very teasing trick. You will be able to keep it going a long time if you work it right. Explain that each person gets three moves, and that after these moves, all of the glasses should be standing in an upright position. Each move consists of picking up any two of the glasses and reversing them. No more and no less than two glasses may be picked up at any one time.

Say to your friends, "I will show you the three moves, and I'll wager you can't repeat them." Then make the three moves, keeping up the patter as you go.

First move: Turn over the second and third glasses, leaving them in the position shown above.

Turn over the first and third glasses, leaving all in the following position: first glass up, second and third down.

For the third and last move, turn over the second and third glasses.

Now all three will be rightside up.

Then give your friends a chance to do the trick, but place the glasses as shown above, which is the reverse of the original position. Naturally, in the final move, all of the glasses will be turned down rather than up, which will mystify them!

Materials: Three glasses placed in a row as shown, the center one up and the outside ones down.

Can you move seven coins from one point to another
on the diagram below without duplicating any moves?

Seven Coins—From Here To There

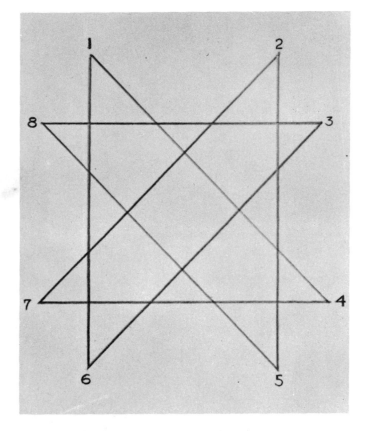

Make a diagram, as shown, on a piece of paper. The numbers are used for practice only. In showing the trick, leave the numbers off, so that no one can keep track of your various moves. Start the first coin anywhere you wish, but move the second coin to the point from which you moved the first one. Repeat the same process with each succeeding coin, then you will not fail. Example: Move from 1 to 6—4 to 1—7 to 4—2 to 7—5 to 2—8 to 5—3 to 8.

Materials: Seven coins, a pencil, and a large sheet of paper.

Can you remove a dime from under a glass without touching it?

THE OBEDIENT COIN

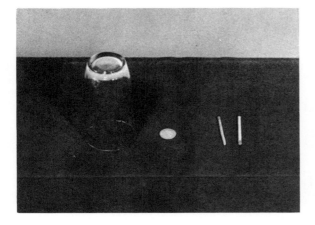

Place a dime or other coin on the table-cloth between the two matches, as shown. Then set the glass upside down on the matches.

The trick is to scratch the tablecloth with the nail of your first finger, near the glass and directly in front of the dime. With rapid, short scratches, draw the fingernail away from the glass and toward yourself.

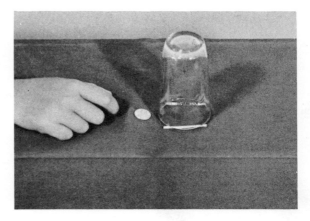

The ripples made by your finger on the tablecloth will cause the dime to move toward you and out from under the glass.

Materials: A glass, a coin, two matches, and a table with a cloth on it.

Do you know how to play the Dickie Bird Game?

Two Little Dickie Birds

This is a cute trick with which you can amuse younger children. You recite a rhyme with it, which goes as follows:

Two little dickie birds sitting on a pole,
One named Peter, and the other named Paul.
Fly away, Peter. Fly away, Paul.
Come back, Peter. Come back, Paul.

Put the adhesive tape on the forefinger of each hand and place the fingers on the edge of the table. Then say, "Two little dickie birds sitting on a pole."

Materials: Two small pieces of adhesive tape.

Raise your right forefinger about three inches as you say, "One named Peter." Replace this finger on the table and raise the left finger, saying "and the other named Paul."

Raise the right hand as you say, "Fly away, Peter."

Bring right hand down, concealing the forefinger and letting the middle finger rest on the table. Do the same thing with your left hand as you say "Fly away, Paul."

The taped fingers, or dickie birds, are now out of sight, and the middle fingers are resting on the table.

Now raise your right hand and say, "Come back, Peter," placing your right forefinger on the table. Then raise your left hand and say, "Come back, Paul," replacing your left forefinger on the table.

Both dickie birds are again sitting on a pole.

Can you make water go *up* into a glass?

THE RISING WATER

Place some water in a saucer, and ask a friend if he can make the water go up into the glass without touching the saucer. When he says it's impossible, show him how it can be done.

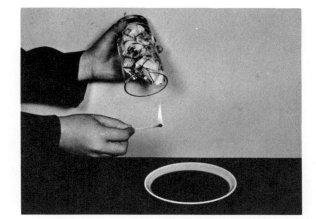

Push the paper into the inverted glass, and light the paper with the match. Wait a few seconds.

Then place the glass in which the paper is burning in the saucer of water. The fire will use up the oxygen in the glass and the water will be drawn up in its place. (A few drops of coloring were added to the water shown here for photographic purposes.)

Materials: A saucer with a small amount of water in it, a glass, a match, a small piece of paper, and a pencil.

Can you guess what was secretly written on a piece of paper?

The Mind-Reading Trick

In the center of the paper, draw a circle not more than one and a half inches across. Hand this to someone in your audience, and tell him to write a short question inside the circle.

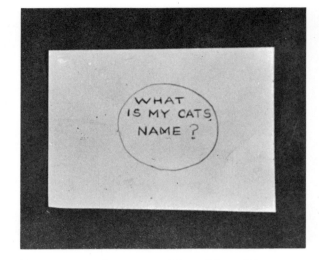

He may write something like this:

Of course you aren't allowed to look at what he has written, but he may pass it around for others to see.

Then tell him to fold the paper twice down the middle—that is, once in each direction as shown.

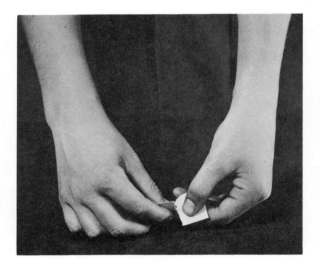

Pick up this folded paper and tear it in half, placing the half with the center corner underneath the other half.

Materials: Piece of paper about three by four inches, pencil, a large ash tray, and a match.

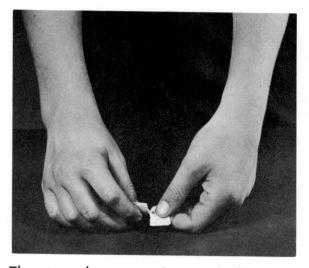

Then tear these two pieces in half again, placing the center corner piece again underneath all the other pieces. Slide the corner piece, which is on the bottom, into the palm of your right hand and hold it there with your little finger while you continue tearing up the other pieces.

Then drop these pieces into a large ash tray, and light them with a match.

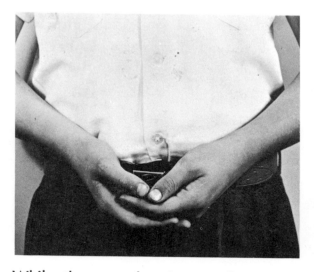

While they are burning, walk around the room and pretend to be concentrating. When your back is turned, open the piece of paper in your right hand and read the message. You must do this quickly, afterwards slipping the paper into your pocket or shirt front.

The message on the paper will look like this:

Now stand again by the ash tray; concentrate over the dying flames and reveal the message or answer the question. You can do some hocus-pocus with your hands over the ash tray to make the trick seem difficult and more magical.

Can you remove the dollar bill without touching or knocking down the bottles?

Another Bill and Bottle Trick

Balance one bottle on top of the other with the bill between as shown. Be sure the bottles are perfectly dry.

Grasp the bill tightly between the thumb and fingers of your left hand. Then with a sharp quick blow strike the bill hard with the forefinger of your right hand, as shown.

The bill will slip out and the bottles remain standing.

Materials: A new crisp dollar bill and two short, stubby bottles.

Can you take away one corner of a square
and thus produce five corners?

Two Corners For One

Hold up the piece of paper
and say, "See, it now has
four corners. Let's give it five!"

Simply cut off one corner, and
you will find you have "two
for one," or a total of
five corners.

Materials: A square piece of paper and a pair of scissors.

Can you add five matches to six matches and make nine?

Five Plus Six Make Nine

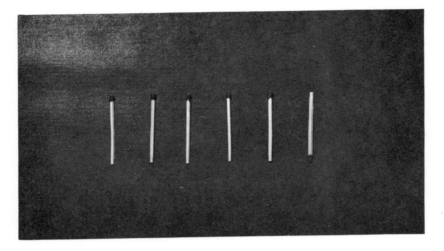

Place six matches on the table so that they form a row as shown. Lay the other five in a pile. Tell your friends to add these five to the other six, without moving the row, and make nine.

If they have not succeeded in a reasonable length of time, tell them that you thought anyone could spell "nine!" Then show them.

Materials: Eleven matches.

Can you lift a pyramid of three matches with a fourth match?

THE PYRAMID TRICK

Slit the untreated end of the first match, and whittle the untreated end of the second match to a flat wedge. Force the wedge of the second match into the slit in the first match. You will now have an inverted V.

Now form the pyramid by standing these joined matches head down on the table and placing the third match head down, so that the end of it rests at the top.

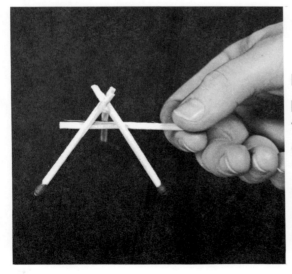

Place the fourth match under the peak of the pyramid. Very gently and slowly, push the two matches that formed the inverted V away from the third match in the pyramid. You will see the third match fall into the throat of the V. Now raise the match which is in your hand, and you will find you can pick up all three.

Materials: Four kitchen matches and a small paring knife. This is a good trick, but it requires a steady hand, and you should practice it before trying it on your friends.

Can you join two pieces of string in your mouth?

THE STRING TRICK

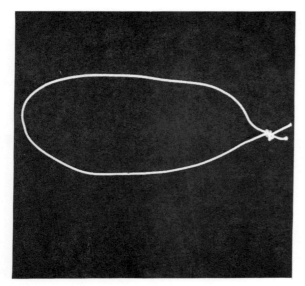

Hold the string up before your friends and knot the two ends together.

Twist the string in one full turn with your hands. This is the part that requires practice. It is important to get just the right twist.

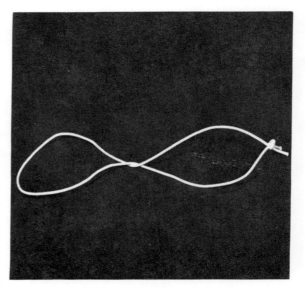

Materials:

A piece of string two or three feet long and a pair of scissors.

Now fold one loop over the other, as shown, put your hands through the double loop and pull taut, holding the "lock" or twisted part between the thumb and first finger of one hand.

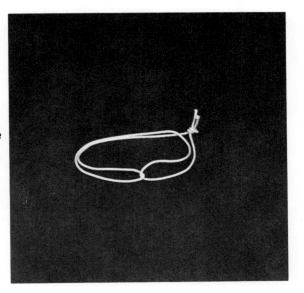

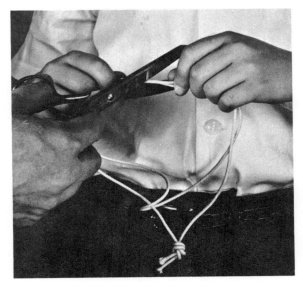

Grasp the string with your left hand a couple of inches away from your right hand, and ask someone to cut through the two strings between your left and right hands.

Now still keeping the "lock" in between thumb and finger of right hand so it does not show, hold up the string to show it has been cut in two.

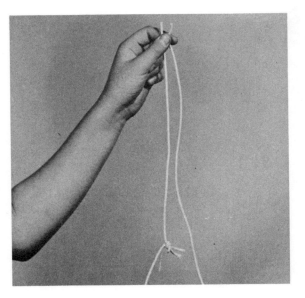

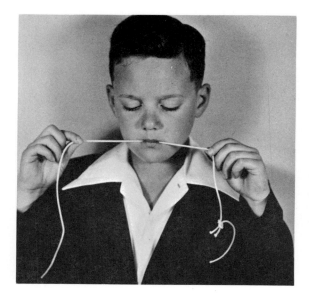

Bring your right hand to your mouth, place the locked part in your mouth. Take hold of the opposite ends with each hand and go through the motion of chewing and let your tongue push the short piece of string to the side of your mouth.

Pull long string out of your mouth, and pass it around. Who can doubt that you joined the two pieces in your mouth?

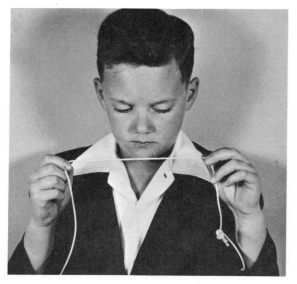

When you have a chance, you can slip the short piece out of your mouth on the sly. It will look like the piece in the picture.

Can you light a match and burn it under water?
Your patter is particularly important in this trick.

Fire Under Water Trick

Simply strike the match on the
bottom of the glass and
keep it under the glass while
it burns. Your friends can't
deny that it is burning
under water!

Materials: Kitchen match and glass partly filled with water.

Would you like to astound your friends with a neat balancing trick?

The Glass and Plate Trick

This trick looks difficult to onlookers because they see it from the front and believe you are doing an extraordinary feat of balancing. It is a good trick to do between other tricks, since it can be done on the spur of the moment.

Place the plate in the right hand with the fingers holding the rim in front toward your audience, and with your thumb in back of the plate, extended upward. Be sure the thumb is not above the edge of the plate, or it will be seen by your friends. Now set the glass carefully on the edge of the plate and support it with your thumb, as shown.

This is how it will look to your friends:

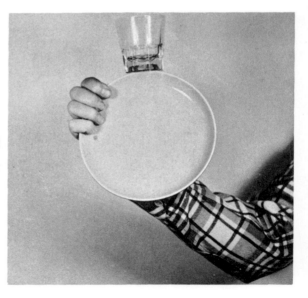

Materials: A plate and a glass.

54

Can you make an egg come out of an empty purse?

THE MAGIC PURSE

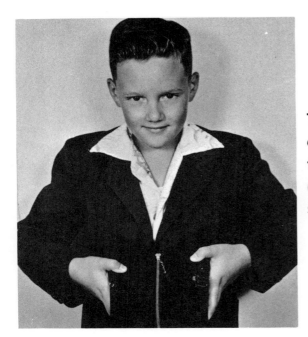

This is a good trick to perform after dinner while your friends are still at the table. You will need a confederate (someone who knows the trick) sitting next to you.

As the purse is passed around the table ask everyone to examine it carefully, turn it upside down, and shake it. A little patter will create interest. When the purse comes to your confederate, he slips in the egg which he has had in his pocket all the time. When the purse comes back to you, say a few magic words and then pull out the egg.

Materials: An empty purse and an egg.
(A hard-boiled egg is safest!)

RANDOM HOUSE BOOKS FOR CHILDREN

Question and Answer Books

For ages 6-10:
Question and Answer Book of Nature
Question and Answer Book of Science
Question and Answer Book of Space
Question and Answer Book About the
   Human Body

Gateway Books

For ages 8 and up:
The Friendly Dolphins
The Horse that Swam Away
Champ: Gallant Collie
Mystery of the Musical Umbrella
and other titles

Step-Up Books

For ages 7-8:
Animals Do the Strangest Things
Birds Do the Strangest Things
Fish Do the Strangest Things
Meet Abraham Lincoln
Meet John F. Kennedy
and other titles

Babar Books

For ages 4 and up:
The Story of Babar
Babar the King
The Travels of Babar
Babar Comes to America
and other titles

Books by Dr. Seuss

For ages 5 and up:
Dr. Seuss's Sleep Book
Happy Birthday to You!
Horton Hatches the Egg
Horton Hears a Who
If I Ran the Zoo
I Had Trouble in Getting to Solla
   Sollew
McElligot's Pool
On Beyond Zebra
Scrambled Eggs Super!
The Sneetches
Thidwick: The Big-Hearted Moose
Yertle the Turtle
and other titles

Giant Picture Books

For ages 5 and up:
Abraham Lincoln
Big Black Horse
Big Book of Things to Do and
   Make
Big Book of Tricks and Magic
Blue Fairy Book
Daniel Boone
Famous Indian Tribes
George Washington
Hiawatha
King Arthur
Peter Pan
Robert E. Lee
Robin Hood
Robinson Crusoe
Three Little Horses
Three Little Horses at the King's
   Palace

Beginner Books

For ages 5-7:
The Cat in the Hat Beginner Book
   Dictionary
The Cat in the Hat
The Cat in the Hat Comes Back
Dr. Seuss's ABC Book
Green Eggs and Ham
Go, Dog, Go!
Bennett Cerf's Book of Riddles
The King, the Mice and the Cheese
and other titles

Picture Books

For ages 4 and up:
Poems to Read to the Very Young
Songs to Sing with the Very Young
Stories to Read to the Very Young
Alice in Wonderland
Anderson's Fairy Tales
Bambi's Children
Black Beauty
Favorite Tales for the Very Young
Grandmas and Grandpas
Grimm's Fairy Tales
Heidi
Little Lost Kitten
Mother Goose
Once-Upon-A-Time Storybook
Pinocchio
Puppy Dog Tales
Read-Aloud Nursery Tales
Sleeping Beauty
The Sleepytime Storybook
Stories that Never Grow Old
The Wild and Wooly Animal Book
The Wizard of Oz

RANDOM HOUSE, INC., 457 MADISON AVENUE, NEW YORK 22, N. Y.